HIGH PROTE.

"40 Nutritious High-Protein Soups Recipes"

ALLIE NAGEL

Copyright © 2024 by Allie Nagel

All rights reserved. No part of this book may be reproduced, stored, or transmitted by any means whether auditory, graphic, mechanical, or electronic without written permission of the author, except in the case of brief excerpts used in critical articles and reviews.

All the people depicted in stock imagery are models, and such images are being used for illustrative purposes only.

DISCLAIMER

This cookbook is intended to provide general information and recipes.

The recipes provided in this cookbook are not intended to replace or be a substitute for medical advice from a physician.

The reader should consult a healthcare professional for any specific medical advice, diagnosis or treatment.

Any specific dietary advice provided in this cookbook is not intended to replace or be a substitute for medical advice from a physician.

The author is not responsible or liable for any adverse effects experienced by readers of this cookbook as a result of following the recipes or dietary advice provided.

The author makes no representations or warranties of any kind (express or implied) as to the accuracy, completeness, reliability or suitability of the recipes provided in this cookbook.

The author disclaims any and all liability for any damages arising out of the use or misuse of the recipes provided in this cookbook. The reader must also take care to ensure that the recipes provided in this cookbook are prepared and cooked safely.

The recipes provided in this cookbook are for informational purposes only and should not be used as a substitute for professional medical advice, diagnosis or treatment.

TABLE OF CONTENTS

INTRODUCTION 7
CHAPTER 1 9
   TIPS FOR MAKING A PLANT BASED SOUP BASE 9
   TIPS FOR MAKING HIGH-PROTEIN BROTHS AND STOCKS 11
   HOW TO BALANCE FLAVORS AND NUTRITION 14
CHAPTER 2 19
   40 NUTRITIOUS HIGH PROTEIN SOUPS RECIPES 19
   PLANT BASED HIGH PROTEIN RECIPES 19
   Lentil and Vegetable Soup 19
   Quinoa and Black Bean Soup 20
   Chickpea and Spinach Stew 22
   Vegan Split Pea Soup 23
   Tuscan White Bean and Kale Soup 24
   Curried Red Lentil Soup 26
   Mushroom and Barley Soup 27
   Thai Coconut Chickpea Soup 29
   Sweet Potato and Black Bean Chili 30
   Spicy Lentil and Tomato Soup 32
   CHICKEN SOUP RECIPES 34
   Classic Chicken Noodle Soup 34
   Lemon Chicken Orzo Soup 35
   Mexican Chicken Tortilla Soup 36
   Thai Coconut Chicken Soup 38
   Chicken and Vegetable Soup 40
   Creamy Chicken and Wild Rice Soup 41
   Moroccan Chicken and Chickpea Soup 43
   Tomato Basil Chicken Soup 44

Chicken and Lentil Soup 46
Creamy Chicken and Mushroom Soup 47
LOW CARB SEAFOOD SOUP 49
Keto Shrimp and Cauliflower Chowder 49
Creamy Garlic Butter Tuscan Shrimp Soup 51
Spicy Low Carb Crab Soup 52
Coconut Lime Seafood Soup 53
Spaghetti Squash and Clam Chowder 55
Thai Coconut Seafood Soup 56
Mediterranean Low Carb Fish Soup 58
Cajun Shrimp and Sausage Gumbo 59
Scallop and Bacon Chowder 61
Lemon Dill Low Carb Salmon Soup 63
VEGETABLE BROTH SOUP RECIPES 64
Classic Vegetable Broth 64
Spinach and White Bean Soup 65
Butternut Squash Soup 67
Mushroom Barley Soup 68
Tomato Basil Soup 69
Kale and Potato Soup 71
High-Protein Cabbage Soup 72
High-Protein Leek and Potato Soup 74
Cauliflower Soup 75
Asparagus and Pea Soup 77
CONCLUSION 79

INTRODUCTION

High-protein soups have emerged as a nourishing and satisfying addition to the culinary world, catering to anyone seeking a protein-packed meal without compromising on taste or health benefits.

These hearty soups, often crafted with a diverse array of ingredients, serve as a delicious way to meet protein requirements while offering a comforting and warming experience.

At the core of high-protein soups are lean protein sources that contribute to muscle development, repair, and overall satiety.

Ingredients such as chicken, turkey, beans, lentils, quinoa, and tofu take center stage, providing an excellent balance of essential amino acids.

This not only supports the body's structural integrity but also aids in weight management by promoting a feeling of fullness, curbing unnecessary snacking.

One of the standout features of high-protein soups is their versatility. From classic chicken noodle to plant-based lentil variations, these soups can be tailored to suit various dietary preferences and restrictions.

The inclusion of vegetables not only enhances flavor but also provides essential vitamins, minerals, and fiber, creating a well-rounded and nutrient-dense meal.

For those pursuing fitness goals or recovering from intense physical activity, high-protein soups serve as a convenient and nourishing option.

They offer a quick and easily digestible source of protein, aiding in muscle recovery and replenishing energy stores.

Additionally, high-protein soups align with the needs of anyone following specific dietary plans, such as low-carb or ketogenic diets, where maintaining an adequate protein intake is crucial.

These soups present a flavorful alternative to traditional protein sources, making adherence to dietary goals more enjoyable.

CHAPTER 1

TIPS FOR MAKING A PLANT BASED SOUP BASE

1. **Start with Flavorful Broths:** Begin your plant-based soup with a rich, vegetable-based broth. Simmering ingredients like onions, carrots, celery, and various herbs creates a robust foundation for your soup.

2. **Mix Up Your Veggies:** Use a variety of colorful vegetables to add diverse flavors, textures, and a spectrum of nutrients to your plant-based soup. Opt. for a mix of leafy greens, root vegetables, and cruciferous veggies.

3. **Incorporate Whole Grains:** Add whole grains like quinoa, brown rice, or barley to boost the nutritional content and make your plant-based soup more filling.

4. **Leverage Legumes:** Beans, lentils, and chickpeas are excellent sources of plant-based protein and fiber. Incorporate them into your soup for added texture and a protein-packed punch.

5. **Embrace Fresh Herbs:** Elevate the flavor profile of your soup with fresh herbs like basil, cilantro, or parsley.
6. **Experiment with Spices:** Spice blends such as cumin, coriander, turmeric, and paprika can add depth and warmth to your plant-based soup. Be adventurous with your spice choices to create a unique flavor profile.
7. **Don't Forget the Umami:** Enhance the savory quality of your soup by adding umami-rich ingredients like mushrooms, tamari, or miso paste.
8. **Balancing Acidity:** A touch of acidity from ingredients like tomatoes or a splash of citrus juice can brighten up the flavors of your plant-based soup.
9. **Creamy Textures Without Dairy:** Achieve creamy textures without dairy by using coconut milk, almond milk, or blending in some soaked cashews for a luxurious finish.
10. **Layer Flavors Gradually:** Allow flavors to develop by layering ingredients gradually. Start with aromatics like onions and garlic, then add vegetables and herbs at different stages.

11. **Mindful Salt Usage:** Be mindful of salt usage; you can always add more later. Consider using sea salt or tamari for additional depth of flavor.

12. **Customize with Toppings:** Offer a customizable experience by providing various toppings like avocado slices, nutritional yeast, or crunchy seeds for added texture and flavor.

13. **Batch Cooking and Freezing:** Make larger quantities and freeze portions for quick and convenient plant-based meals on busy days.

14. **Add Greens Towards the End:** To preserve their color and nutrients, add leafy greens like spinach or kale towards the end of the cooking process.

15. **Garnish for Visual Appeal:** Garnish your plant-based soup with a drizzle of olive oil, a sprinkle of fresh herbs, or a dash of paprika for a visually appealing and appetizing finish.

TIPS FOR MAKING HIGH-PROTEIN BROTHS AND STOCKS

1. **Choose Protein-Rich Base Ingredients:** Begin with a protein-rich foundation by using ingredients like

bones, chicken carcasses, or plant-based sources like lentils and legumes.

2. **Bone Broth for Animal Protein:** If using animal products, simmer bones for an extended period to extract collagen and protein, creating a nutrient-dense bone broth.

3. **Plant-Based Broths:** For plant-based options, combine protein-packed ingredients like beans, lentils, or quinoa to form a hearty and nutritious base.

4. **Add Aromatics for Depth:** Enhance flavor by including aromatic vegetables such as onions, carrots, celery, garlic, and leeks. These add depth to your high-protein broth.

5. **Utilize Herbs and Spices:** Infuse your broth with herbs like thyme, rosemary, or bay leaves, along with spices such as peppercorns and coriander, to elevate the overall taste.

6. **Acidity for Balance:** Introduce a touch of acidity with ingredients like tomatoes or a splash of vinegar to balance the richness of the broth.

7. **Simmer Slowly for Maximum Extraction:** Allow the broth to simmer slowly over low heat to extract

proteins, collagen, and flavors, resulting in a more robust and nutrient-dense stock.

8. **Skim Off Impurities:** Regularly skim off impurities and foam that rise to the surface during the simmering process for a cleaner and clearer broth.

9. **Experiment with Umami Boosters:** Enhance the savory profile with umami-rich ingredients like dried mushrooms, seaweed, or miso paste for an extra depth of flavor.

10. **Add Protein-Rich Vegetables:** Include protein-rich vegetables like broccoli, spinach, or kale in the broth to boost the overall protein content.

11. **Customize with Proteins of Choice:** Tailor your broth to your dietary preferences by incorporating proteins of choice, such as chicken, beef, tofu, or a combination for a more complex flavor profile.

12. **Use High-Quality Ingredients:** Opt. for high-quality, fresh ingredients to maximize the nutritional value of your broth and achieve a more flavorful result.

13. **Consider Collagen Supplements:** For an additional protein and collagen boost, consider adding collagen supplements to your broth for added health benefits.
14. **Strain Thoroughly:** Strain the broth thoroughly to remove any solids and achieve a clear, smooth liquid that showcases the purity of your high-protein stock.
15. **Portion and Freeze:** Portion the broth into containers and freeze for convenient use in future recipes, ensuring you always have a protein-rich base readily available.

HOW TO BALANCE FLAVORS AND NUTRITION

1. **Incorporate a Variety of Proteins:** Balance flavor and nutrition by incorporating a variety of proteins such as lean meats, poultry, fish, legumes, and plant-based sources. This not only diversifies the taste but also ensures a complete amino acid profile.
2. **Experiment with Broths:** Use flavorful broths as a base, whether they are vegetable, chicken, or bone broth. The broth serves as a foundation for your high-

protein soup, adding depth and richness to the overall flavor.

3. **Optimize Seasonings:** Fine-tune the taste with a well-balanced blend of seasonings, including herbs, spices, and aromatics. Experiment with combinations like thyme and rosemary for a savory profile or cumin and coriander for a hint of warmth.

4. **Mindful Salt Usage:** Use salt judiciously and consider alternatives like sea salt or tamari. Be cautious not to oversalt, as it can overpower the flavors and compromise the nutritional balance.

5. **Leverage Umami-Boosting Ingredients:** Enhance the umami factor with ingredients like mushrooms, soy sauce, miso paste, or nutritional yeast. These additions contribute depth and a savory taste to your high-protein soup.

6. **Add Acid for Brightness:** Balance the richness of the soup with a touch of acidity. Ingredients like tomatoes, lemon juice, or vinegar can brighten the flavors and add a refreshing element.

7. **Include Colorful Vegetables:** Boost both nutrition and visual appeal by incorporating a rainbow of

vegetables. Different colors often indicate a variety of nutrients, ensuring a well-rounded nutritional profile.

8. **Layer Ingredients Gradually:** Build layers of flavor by adding ingredients gradually. Start with aromatic vegetables, followed by proteins, grains, and finally delicate herbs towards the end of cooking for a nuanced taste.

9. **Consider Healthy Fats:** Integrate healthy fats such as olive oil or avocado to enhance mouthfeel and flavor. These fats not only contribute to a satisfying texture but also provide essential nutrients.

10. **Balance Macronutrients:** Ensure a well-balanced macronutrient profile with an appropriate ratio of proteins, carbohydrates, and fats. This helps in creating a satiating and nutritionally dense high-protein soup.

11. **Choose Whole Grains Wisely:** If incorporating grains, choose whole grains like quinoa, brown rice, or barley. These not only add texture but also provide additional nutrients, contributing to a balanced soup.

12. **Customize with Toppings:** Allow for personalization by offering a variety of toppings like fresh herbs, sliced avocado, or crunchy seeds. These toppings not only add texture but also contribute to the overall flavor profile.

13. **Adjust Spices to Taste:** Experiment with spices but be mindful of individual preferences. Adjust the spice levels according to taste, allowing for a personalized and enjoyable experience.

14. **Avoid Overcooking Vegetables:** Maintain the nutritional value of vegetables by avoiding overcooking. Vegetables should be cooked until they are tender yet still vibrant in color and flavor.

15. **Taste and Adjust:** Regularly taste the soup as it simmers and adjust seasonings accordingly. This allows you to fine-tune the flavors and ensure a harmonious balance between taste and nutrition in your high-protein soup.

CHAPTER 3

40 NUTRITIOUS HIGH PROTEIN SOUPS RECIPES s

PLANT BASED HIGH PROTEIN RECIPES

Lentil and Vegetable Soup

Preparation Time: 40 minutes

Serves: 4

Calories: 250

Ingredients:

1 cup dried lentils

4 cups vegetable broth

1 onion, chopped

2 carrots, diced

2 celery stalks, chopped

3 cloves garlic, minced

1 can (14 oz) diced tomatoes

1 teaspoon cumin

1 teaspoon paprika

Salt and pepper

2 cups kale, chopped

Method of Preparation:

1. Rinse lentils and combine with vegetable broth in a pot.
2. Add chopped onion, carrots, celery, garlic, diced tomatoes, cumin, paprika, salt, and pepper.
3. Simmer for 25-30 minutes until lentils are tender.
4. Stir in chopped kale and cook for an additional 5 minutes.

Quinoa and Black Bean Soup

Preparation Time: 35 minutes

Serves: 4

Calories: 300

Ingredients:

1 cup quinoa, rinsed

4 cups vegetable broth

1 onion, finely chopped

2 bell peppers, diced

1 can (15 oz) black beans, drained and rinsed

1 can (14 oz) diced tomatoes

1 teaspoon cumin

1 teaspoon chili powder

Salt and pepper

1 cup corn kernels

Method of Preparation:

1. Combine quinoa, vegetable broth, chopped onion, bell peppers, black beans, diced tomatoes, cumin, chili powder, salt, and pepper in a pot.
2. Bring to a boil, then reduce heat and simmer for 20-25 minutes until quinoa is cooked.

3. Stir in corn kernels and cook for an additional 5 minutes.

Chickpea and Spinach Stew

Preparation Time: 30 minutes

Serves: 4

Calories: 280

Ingredients:

2 cans (15 oz each) chickpeas, drained and rinsed

4 cups vegetable broth

1 onion, chopped

3 cloves garlic, minced

1 teaspoon ground coriander

1 teaspoon smoked paprika

Salt and pepper

4 cups fresh spinach

Juice of 1 lemon

Method of Preparation:

1. In a pot, combine chickpeas, vegetable broth, chopped onion, minced garlic, ground coriander, smoked paprika, salt, and pepper.
2. Simmer for 15-20 minutes.
3. Stir in fresh spinach and cook until wilted.
4. Finish with lemon juice before Serves.

Vegan Split Pea Soup

Preparation Time: 1 hour

Serves: 4

Calories: 250

Ingredients:

1 cup dried split peas

1 onion, diced

2 carrots, chopped

2 celery stalks, chopped

3 cloves garlic, minced

6 cups vegetable broth

1 teaspoon dried thyme

1 bay leaf

Salt and pepper

Method of Preparation:

1. Rinse split peas under cold water.
2. In a large pot, sauté onions, carrots, and celery until softened.
3. Add garlic and cook for another minute.
4. Add split peas, vegetable broth, thyme, bay leaf, salt, and pepper.
5. Bring to a boil, then reduce heat and simmer for 45-60 minutes or until peas are tender.
6. Remove bay leaf, adjust seasoning, and serve.

Tuscan White Bean and Kale Soup

Preparation Time: 30 minutes

Serves: 6

Calories: 200

Ingredients:

2 cans white beans, drained and rinsed

1 onion, finely chopped

3 cloves garlic, minced

1 carrot, diced

1 celery stalk, diced

4 cups vegetable broth

1 can diced tomatoes

2 cups kale, chopped

1 teaspoon dried rosemary

Salt and pepper

Method of Preparation:

1. In a pot, sauté onions, garlic, carrot, and celery until softened.
2. Add white beans, vegetable broth, diced tomatoes, and rosemary.
3. Bring to a simmer and let it cook for 15-20 minutes.
4. Stir in kale and cook until wilted.

5. Season with salt and pepper, then serve.

Curried Red Lentil Soup

Preparation Time: 40 minutes

Serves: 5

Calories: 300

Ingredients:

1 cup red lentils, rinsed

1 onion, diced

2 carrots, sliced

3 cloves garlic, minced

1 tablespoon curry powder

4 cups vegetable broth

1 can coconut milk

1 teaspoon cumin

Salt and pepper

Method of Preparation:

1. Sauté onions, carrots, and garlic until softened.
2. Add curry powder and cook for 1-2 minutes.
3. Add red lentils, vegetable broth, coconut milk, and cumin.
4. Bring to a boil, then simmer for 20-25 minutes or until lentils are tender.
5. Season with salt and pepper, then serve.

Mushroom and Barley Soup

Preparation Time: 1 hour

Serves: 6

Calories: 250

Ingredients:

1 cup barley

8 cups vegetable broth

2 cups sliced mushrooms

1 onion, finely chopped

3 carrots, diced

3 celery stalks, chopped

3 cloves garlic, minced

1 tsp dried thyme

1 tsp dried rosemary

Salt and pepper

2 tbsp olive oil

Fresh parsley for garnish

Method of Preparation:

1. In a large pot, heat olive oil and sauté onions and garlic until fragrant.
2. Add mushrooms, carrots, and celery.
3. Cook until vegetables are slightly softened.
4. Pour in vegetable broth, add barley, thyme, rosemary, salt, and pepper.
5. Bring to a boil, then reduce heat and simmer for 40-45 minutes or until barley is tender.
6. Adjust seasoning if needed and serve hot, garnished with fresh parsley.

Thai Coconut Chickpea Soup

Preparation Time: 30 minutes

Serves: 4

Calories: 320

Ingredients:

1 can (15 oz) chickpeas, drained and rinsed

1 can (14 oz) coconut milk

4 cups vegetable broth

1 red bell pepper, sliced

1 cup snap peas, trimmed

1 lemongrass stalk, smashed

3 tbsp red curry paste

2 tbsp soy sauce

1 tbsp ginger, grated

2 cloves garlic, minced

2 tbsp lime juice

Fresh cilantro for garnish

Method of Preparation:

1. In a large pot, combine coconut milk, vegetable broth, red curry paste, lemongrass, ginger, and garlic.
2. Bring to a simmer.
3. Add chickpeas, red bell pepper, and snap peas.
4. Cook until vegetables are tender.
5. Stir in soy sauce and lime juice.
6. Adjust seasoning to taste.
7. Remove lemongrass stalk and discard.
8. Serve hot, garnished with fresh cilantro.

Sweet Potato and Black Bean Chili

Preparation Time: 40 minutes

Serves: 4-6

Calories: 300

Ingredients:

1 tablespoon olive oil

1 onion, diced

3 cloves garlic, minced

1-pound sweet potatoes, peeled and diced

1 can (15 oz) black beans, drained and rinsed

1 can (14 oz) diced tomatoes

1 cup corn kernels (fresh or frozen)

2 teaspoons chili powder

1 teaspoon cumin

1/2 teaspoon smoked paprika

Salt and pepper

4 cups vegetable broth

1 cup water

Optional toppings: chopped green onions, cilantro, Greek yogurt

Method of Preparation:

1. In a large pot, heat olive oil over medium heat.
2. Add onions and garlic, sauté until softened.

3. Add sweet potatoes, black beans, diced tomatoes, corn, chili powder, cumin, smoked paprika, salt, and pepper.
4. Stir well.
5. Pour in vegetable broth and water.
6. Bring to a boil, then reduce heat and simmer for 20-25 minutes or until sweet potatoes are tender.
7. Adjust seasoning if needed.
8. Serve hot, topped with green onions, cilantro, and a dollop of Greek yogurt if desired.

Spicy Lentil and Tomato Soup

Preparation Time: 45 minutes

Serves: 4-6

Calories: 250

Ingredients:

1 tablespoon olive oil

1 onion, finely chopped

2 carrots, diced

2 celery stalks, chopped

3 cloves garlic, minced

1 cup dried lentils, rinsed

1 can (14 oz) diced tomatoes

1 teaspoon cumin

1/2 teaspoon coriander

1/4 teaspoon cayenne pepper (adjust to taste)

6 cups vegetable broth

Salt and pepper

Fresh parsley for garnish

Method of Preparation:

1. In a large pot, heat olive oil over medium heat. Add onions, carrots, celery, and garlic.
2. Sauté until vegetables are softened.
3. Add lentils, diced tomatoes, cumin, coriander, cayenne pepper, vegetable broth, salt, and pepper. Stir well.
4. Bring to a boil, then reduce heat and simmer for 25-30 minutes or until lentils are tender.
5. Adjust seasoning if needed.

6. Serve hot, garnished with fresh parsley.

CHICKEN SOUP RECIPES

Classic Chicken Noodle Soup

Preparation Time: 30 minutes

Serves: 6

Calories: 250

Ingredients:

1 lb. boneless, skinless chicken breasts

8 cups chicken broth (low-sodium)

2 carrots, sliced

2 celery stalks, chopped

1 onion, diced

3 cloves garlic, minced

2 cups egg noodles

1 tsp dried thyme

Salt and pepper

Method of Preparation:

1. In a large pot, bring chicken broth to a simmer.
2. Add chicken breasts and cook until done. Remove, shred, and set aside.
3. In the same pot, sauté onions, garlic, carrots, and celery until softened.
4. Add shredded chicken, egg noodles, thyme, salt, and pepper.
5. Simmer until noodles are cooked.
6. Adjust seasoning as needed.

Lemon Chicken Orzo Soup

Preparation Time: 35 minutes

Serves: 5

Calories: 280

Ingredients:

1 lb. boneless, skinless chicken thighs

8 cups chicken broth (low-sodium)

1 cup orzo pasta

2 carrots, diced

2 celery stalks, sliced

1 onion, finely chopped

Zest and juice of 2 lemons

1 tsp dried oregano

Salt and pepper

Method of Preparation:

1. In a pot, bring chicken broth to a boil, add chicken thighs, and cook until done. Remove, shred, and set aside.
2. In the same pot, add orzo, carrots, celery, onion, lemon zest, lemon juice, oregano, salt, and pepper.
3. Simmer until orzo is cooked and veggies are tender.
4. Stir in shredded chicken and serve.

Mexican Chicken Tortilla Soup

Preparation Time: 40 minutes

Serves: 6

Calories: 300

Ingredients:

1 lb. boneless, skinless chicken thighs

8 cups chicken broth (low-sodium)

1 can black beans, drained and rinsed

1 cup corn kernels

1 bell pepper, diced

1 onion, chopped

3 cloves garlic, minced

1 can diced tomatoes

1 tsp ground cumin

1 tsp chili powder

Salt and pepper

Tortilla strips for garnish

Method of Preparation:

1. In a pot, bring chicken broth to a boil, add chicken thighs, and cook until done.
2. Remove, shred, and set aside.

3. In the same pot, add black beans, corn, bell pepper, onion, garlic, diced tomatoes, cumin, chili powder, salt, and pepper.
4. Simmer until veggies are tender.
5. Stir in shredded chicken.
6. Serve with tortilla strips on top.

Thai Coconut Chicken Soup

Preparation time: 30 minutes

Serves: 4

Calories: 300

Ingredients:

1 lb. boneless, skinless chicken breast, diced

1 can (14 oz) coconut milk

4 cups chicken broth

1 cup sliced mushrooms

1 red bell pepper, thinly sliced

1 stalk lemongrass, crushed

3 kaffir lime leaves

2 tablespoons fish sauce

1 tablespoon grated ginger

1 tablespoon red curry paste

1 tablespoon coconut oil

Fresh cilantro and lime wedges for garnish

Method of Preparation:

1. In a pot, heat coconut oil over medium heat.
2. Add red curry paste and grated ginger, sauté for 2 minutes.
3. Add diced chicken, cook until browned.
4. Pour in coconut milk and chicken broth.
5. Add lemongrass, kaffir lime leaves, mushrooms, and red bell pepper.
6. Simmer for 15-20 minutes.
7. Stir in fish sauce and simmer for an additional 5 minutes.
8. Remove lemongrass and kaffir lime leaves before Serves. Garnish with fresh cilantro and lime wedges.

Chicken and Vegetable Soup

Preparation time: 40 minutes

Serves: 6

Calories: 250

Ingredients:

1 lb. boneless, skinless chicken thighs, shredded

6 cups chicken broth

2 carrots, sliced

2 celery stalks, chopped

1 onion, diced

2 garlic cloves, minced

1 cup green beans, cut into bite-sized pieces

1 teaspoon dried thyme

Salt and pepper

1 tablespoon olive oil

Fresh parsley for garnish

Method of Preparation:

1. In a large pot, heat olive oil over medium heat.
2. Sauté onions and garlic until softened.
3. Add shredded chicken, carrots, celery, and green beans.
4. Cook for 5 minutes.
5. Pour in chicken broth, add dried thyme, salt, and pepper.
6. Bring to a boil, then simmer for 20-25 minutes.
7. Garnish with fresh parsley before Serves.

Creamy Chicken and Wild Rice Soup

Preparation time: 50 minutes

Serves: 5

Calories: 350

Ingredients:

1 lb. boneless, skinless chicken breasts, cubed

1 cup wild rice, uncooked

6 cups chicken broth

1 cup sliced carrots

1 cup sliced celery

1 onion, finely chopped

2 cloves garlic, minced

1 cup heavy cream

2 tablespoons all-purpose flour

3 tablespoons butter

Salt and pepper

Fresh thyme for garnish

Method of Preparation:

1. In a pot, melt butter over medium heat.
2. Sauté onions and garlic until translucent.
3. Add chicken, cook until browned.
4. Sprinkle flour over the chicken and stir.
5. Pour in chicken broth, add wild rice, carrots, and celery.
6. Simmer for 30-40 minutes until rice is cooked.
7. Stir in heavy cream, season with salt and pepper. Simmer for an additional 10 minutes.

8. Garnish with fresh thyme before Serves.

Moroccan Chicken and Chickpea Soup

Preparation Time: 40 minutes

Serves: 4

Calories: 350

Ingredients:

1 lb. boneless, skinless chicken breasts, diced

1 cup dried chickpeas, soaked and cooked

1 large onion, finely chopped

3 cloves garlic, minced

2 carrots, diced

2 celery stalks, chopped

1 can (14 oz) diced tomatoes

1/2 cup tomato paste

1 tsp ground cumin

1 tsp ground coriander

1 tsp smoked paprika

1/2 tsp cinnamon

6 cups chicken broth

Salt and pepper

Fresh cilantro for garnish

Method of Preparation:

1. In a large pot, sauté onions and garlic until translucent.
2. Add diced chicken and cook until browned.
3. Stir in carrots, celery, diced tomatoes, tomato paste, cumin, coriander, smoked paprika, and cinnamon.
4. Pour in chicken broth, add cooked chickpeas, and season with salt and pepper.
5. Simmer for 20-25 minutes until vegetables are tender and flavors meld.
6. Garnish with fresh cilantro before Serves.

Tomato Basil Chicken Soup

Preparation Time: 35 minutes

Serves: 6

Calories: 250

Ingredients:

1 lb. boneless, skinless chicken thighs, shredded

1 onion, finely chopped

3 cloves garlic, minced

4 cups fresh tomatoes, diced

2 cups chicken broth

1 can (14 oz) crushed tomatoes

1/2 cup fresh basil, chopped

1 tsp dried oregano

Salt and pepper

2 tbsp olive oil

Method of Preparation:

1. In a pot, sauté onions and garlic in olive oil until softened.

2. Add shredded chicken and cook until lightly browned.
3. Stir in fresh tomatoes, crushed tomatoes, chicken broth, basil, oregano, salt, and pepper.
4. Simmer for 25-30 minutes to allow flavors to meld.
5. Adjust seasoning as needed and serve hot.

Chicken and Lentil Soup

Preparation Time: 30 minutes

Serves: 4

Calories: 300

Ingredients:

1 lb. boneless, skinless chicken breast, diced

1 cup dried green or brown lentils, rinsed

1 onion, diced

2 carrots, sliced

2 celery stalks, chopped

3 cloves garlic, minced

1 teaspoon cumin

1 teaspoon paprika

6 cups low-sodium chicken broth

Salt and pepper

Fresh parsley for garnish

Method of Preparation:

1. In a large pot, sauté chicken until browned.
2. Add onions, carrots, celery, and garlic, cooking until vegetables are softened.
3. Stir in cumin and paprika, then add lentils and chicken broth.
4. Bring to a boil, then reduce heat and simmer until lentils are tender.
5. Season with Salt and pepper.
6. Garnish with fresh parsley before Serves.

Creamy Chicken and Mushroom Soup

Preparation Time: 40 minutes

Serves: 4

Calories: 400

Ingredients:

1 lb. boneless, skinless chicken thighs, diced

8 oz mushrooms, sliced

1 onion, finely chopped

3 cloves garlic, minced

4 cups chicken broth

1 cup heavy cream

2 tablespoons butter

2 tablespoons all-purpose flour

Salt and pepper

Fresh thyme for garnish

Method of Preparation:

1. In a pot, cook chicken until browned.
2. Add butter, onions, garlic, and mushrooms.
3. Cook until vegetables are tender.

4. Sprinkle flour over the mixture, stirring constantly. Gradually add chicken broth, then bring to a simmer.
5. Stir in heavy cream and let it simmer until the soup thickens. Season with salt and pepper.
6. Garnish with fresh thyme before Serves.

LOW CARB SEAFOOD SOUP

Keto Shrimp and Cauliflower Chowder

Preparation Time: 30 minutes

Serves: 4

Calories: 380

Ingredients:

1 lb. shrimp, peeled and deveined

1 medium cauliflower, chopped

4 cups chicken broth

1 cup heavy cream

1 cup shredded cheddar cheese

4 slices bacon, cooked and crumbled

3 cloves garlic, minced

1 onion, diced

2 tbsp butter

2 tsp thyme

Salt and pepper

Method of Preparation:

1. In a large pot, melt butter and sauté garlic and onion until softened.
2. Add chicken broth, cauliflower, and thyme.
3. Simmer until cauliflower is tender.
4. Blend half of the soup until smooth and return to the pot.
5. Stir in heavy cream, shrimp, and shredded cheese.
6. Cook until shrimp turn pink.
7. Season with salt and pepper.
8. Serve hot, garnished with crumbled bacon.

Creamy Garlic Butter Tuscan Shrimp Soup

Preparation Time: 25 minutes

Serves: 4

Calories: 420

Ingredients:

1 lb. shrimp, peeled and deveined

1 cup cherry tomatoes, halved

4 cups chicken broth

1 cup heavy cream

3 tbsp butter

4 cloves garlic, minced

1 cup spinach, chopped

1/2 cup grated Parmesan cheese

Salt and pepper

Fresh basil for garnish

Method of Preparation:

1. In a pot, melt butter and sauté garlic until fragrant.
2. Add chicken broth and bring to a simmer.
3. Add shrimp and cook until pink.
4. Stir in heavy cream, cherry tomatoes, spinach, and Parmesan cheese.
5. Simmer until heated through.
6. Season with salt and pepper.
7. Garnish with fresh basil before Serves.

Spicy Low Carb Crab Soup

Preparation Time: 20 minutes

Serves: 4

Calories: 280

Ingredients:

1 lb. lump crab meat

4 cups chicken broth

1 cup coconut milk

1 red bell pepper, diced

2 stalks celery, sliced

1 tbsp ginger, minced

2 cloves garlic, minced

1 tsp chili flakes (adjust to taste)

2 tbsp coconut oil

Salt and pepper

Fresh cilantro for garnish

Method of Preparation:

1. In a pot, sauté ginger, garlic, red bell pepper, and celery in coconut oil until softened.
2. Add chicken broth and bring to a simmer.
3. Stir in coconut milk and crab meat.
4. Season with chili flakes, salt, and pepper.
5. Simmer until heated through.
6. Garnish with fresh cilantro before Serves.

Coconut Lime Seafood Soup

Preparation Time: 30 minutes

Serves: 4

Calories: 300

Ingredients:

1 lb. mixed seafood (shrimp, mussels, and/or fish)

1 can (13.5 oz) coconut milk

3 cups fish or vegetable broth

1 stalk lemongrass, sliced

1 red bell pepper, thinly sliced

1 tablespoon ginger, minced

2 cloves garlic, minced

Zest and juice of 2 limes

1 tablespoon fish sauce

Salt and pepper

Fresh cilantro for garnish

Method of Preparation:

1. In a large pot, combine coconut milk, broth, lemongrass, ginger, and garlic.
2. Bring to a simmer.

3. Add mixed seafood and sliced bell pepper.
4. Cook until seafood is cooked through.
5. Stir in lime zest, lime juice, and fish sauce.
6. Season with salt and pepper.
7. Serve hot, garnished with fresh cilantro.

Spaghetti Squash and Clam Chowder

Preparation Time: 45 minutes

Serves: 4

Calories: 250

Ingredients:

1 medium spaghetti squash

2 cans (6.5 oz each) minced clams, drained

3 cups vegetable broth

1 cup celery, chopped

1 cup onion, diced

1 cup cauliflower, chopped

2 cloves garlic, minced

1 teaspoon dried thyme

1 cup unsweetened almond milk

Salt and pepper

Fresh parsley for garnish

Method of Preparation:

1. Roast spaghetti squash in the oven until tender.
2. Scrape out the strands.
3. In a pot, sauté celery, onion, and garlic until softened.
4. Add cauliflower and vegetable broth. Simmer until cauliflower is tender.
5. Stir in minced clams, thyme, almond milk, and spaghetti squash strands.
6. Season with salt and pepper.
7. Simmer until heated through.
8. Garnish with fresh parsley.

Thai Coconut Seafood Soup

Preparation Time: 25 minutes

Serves: 4

Calories: 320

Ingredients:

1 lb. mixed seafood (shrimp, squid, and/or scallops)

1 can (14 oz) coconut milk

4 cups chicken or vegetable broth

2 tablespoons red curry paste

1 tablespoon fish sauce

1 tablespoon soy sauce

1 tablespoon lime juice

1 tablespoon brown sugar

1 red chili, sliced (optional)

Fresh cilantro and lime wedges for garnish

Method of Preparation:

1. In a pot, combine coconut milk, broth, red curry paste, fish sauce, soy sauce, and brown sugar.
2. Bring to a simmer.
3. Add mixed seafood and cook until done.

4. Stir in lime juice.
5. Garnish with sliced red chili, fresh cilantro, and lime wedges.

Mediterranean Low Carb Fish Soup

Preparation Time: 30 minutes

Serves: 4

Calories: 250

Ingredients:

1 lb. white fish fillets (such as cod or halibut), cut into chunks

1 onion, finely chopped

2 cloves garlic, minced

1 can (14 oz) diced tomatoes, undrained

1 zucchini, diced

1 bell pepper, chopped

1/4 cup olives, sliced

1 tablespoon olive oil

4 cups fish or vegetable broth

1 teaspoon dried oregano

1 teaspoon dried thyme

Salt and pepper

Fresh parsley for garnish

Method of Preparation:

1. In a large pot, heat olive oil over medium heat.
2. Add onions and garlic, sauté until softened.
3. Add diced tomatoes, zucchini, bell pepper, and olives.
4. Stir in fish broth.
5. Bring the mixture to a simmer, then add fish chunks, oregano, thyme, salt, and pepper.
6. Simmer for about 15-20 minutes until the fish is cooked through.
7. Garnish with fresh parsley before Serves.

Cajun Shrimp and Sausage Gumbo

Preparation Time: 45 minutes

Serves: 6

Calories: 400

Ingredients:

1 lb. shrimp, peeled and deveined

1 lb. andouille sausage, sliced

1 onion, diced

1 bell pepper, diced

2 celery stalks, chopped

3 cloves garlic, minced

1/4 cup all-purpose flour (or almond flour for low-carb)

1/4 cup vegetable oil

4 cups chicken broth

1 can (14 oz) diced tomatoes, undrained

1 teaspoon Cajun seasoning

1 teaspoon dried thyme

Salt and pepper

Green onions for garnish

Method of Preparation:

1. In a large pot, make a roux by whisking flour and oil over medium heat until browned.
2. Add onions, bell pepper, celery, and garlic.
3. Sauté until vegetables are softened.
4. Stir in chicken broth, diced tomatoes, Cajun seasoning, thyme, salt, and pepper.
5. Bring to a boil, then reduce heat and simmer for 20 minutes.
6. Add shrimp and sausage, cook until shrimp are pink and sausage is heated through.
7. Garnish with green onions before Serves.

Scallop and Bacon Chowder

Preparation Time: 30 minutes

Serves: 4

Calories: 350

Ingredients:

1 lb. scallops, cleaned and halved

6 slices of lean bacon, diced

1 onion, finely chopped

2 cloves garlic, minced

3 cups cauliflower florets

4 cups chicken broth

1 cup heavy cream

1 tsp thyme

Salt and pepper

Chopped fresh parsley for garnish

Method of Preparation:

1. In a large pot, cook diced bacon until crispy.
2. Remove bacon and set aside.
3. Sauté onion and garlic in bacon fat until softened.
4. Add cauliflower, chicken broth, and thyme.
5. Simmer until cauliflower is tender.
6. Stir in scallops, heavy cream, and cooked bacon. Cook until scallops are just opaque.
7. Season with salt and pepper.
8. Garnish with chopped parsley before Serves.

Lemon Dill Low Carb Salmon Soup

Preparation Time: 25 minutes

Serves: 4

Calories: 280

Ingredients:

1 lb. skinless salmon fillets, diced

1 tbsp olive oil

1 onion, finely chopped

3 celery stalks, diced

1 leek, sliced

4 cups fish or vegetable broth

Juice of 2 lemons

1 tsp dried dill

Salt and pepper

1 cup spinach, chopped

1/2 cup heavy cream (optional)

Method of Preparation:

1. In a large pot, sauté onions, celery, and leek in olive oil until softened.
2. Add diced salmon, broth, lemon juice, and dried dill. Simmer until salmon is cooked.
3. Season with salt and pepper.
4. Stir in chopped spinach and heavy cream if using.
5. Simmer for an additional 5 minutes.
6. Adjust seasoning if needed.

VEGETABLE BROTH SOUP RECIPES

Classic Vegetable Broth

Preparation Time: 45 minutes

Serves: 6

Calories: 50

Ingredients:

1 onion, chopped

2 carrots, sliced

2 celery stalks, chopped

1 leek, sliced

3 cloves garlic, minced

1 bay leaf

1 teaspoon dried thyme

1 teaspoon dried rosemary

8 cups vegetable broth (low-sodium)

Salt and pepper

Method of Preparation:

1. In a large pot, sauté onions, carrots, celery, leek, and garlic until softened.
2. Add bay leaf, thyme, rosemary, and vegetable broth. Bring to a boil.
3. Reduce heat, cover, and simmer for 30-40 minutes.
4. Season with Salt and pepper.
5. Strain the broth, discarding the solids.

Spinach and White Bean Soup

Preparation Time: 30 minutes

Serves: 4

Calories: 180

Ingredients:

1 tablespoon olive oil

1 onion, diced

2 cloves garlic, minced

1 can (15 oz) white beans, drained and rinsed

4 cups vegetable broth (low-sodium)

4 cups fresh spinach

1 teaspoon dried thyme

Salt and pepper

Method of Preparation:

1. In a large pot, heat olive oil and sauté onion and garlic until translucent.
2. Add white beans, vegetable broth, thyme, salt, and pepper.
3. Bring to a simmer.
4. Stir in fresh spinach and cook until wilted.
5. Simmer for an additional 10-15 minutes.

Butternut Squash Soup

Preparation Time: 40 minutes

Serves: 6

Calories: 150

Ingredients:

1 butternut squash, peeled, seeded, and cubed

1 onion, chopped

2 carrots, chopped

2 apples, peeled, cored, and chopped

4 cups vegetable broth (low-sodium)

1 teaspoon ground cinnamon

1/2 teaspoon nutmeg

Salt and pepper

1/2 cup Greek yogurt (as a healthy alternative to cream)

Method of Preparation:

1. In a large pot, combine butternut squash, onion, carrots, apples, and vegetable broth.
2. Bring to a boil.
3. Reduce heat and simmer until vegetables are tender.
4. Puree the soup using an immersion blender until smooth.
5. Stir in cinnamon, nutmeg, salt, and pepper.
6. Serve with a dollop of Greek yogurt.

Mushroom Barley Soup

Preparation Time: 40 minutes

Serves: 4

Calories: 250

Ingredients:

1 cup barley

8 cups vegetable broth

2 cups mushrooms, sliced

1 onion, diced

2 carrots, sliced

2 celery stalks, chopped

3 cloves garlic, minced

1 teaspoon thyme

Salt and pepper

2 tablespoons olive oil

Method of Preparation:

1. In a large pot, heat olive oil and sauté onions and garlic until softened.
2. Add mushrooms, carrots, and celery, cooking until vegetables are tender.
3. Pour in vegetable broth, barley, thyme, salt, and pepper.
4. Bring to a boil, then simmer until barley is cooked.
5. Adjust seasoning if needed.
6. Serve hot.

Tomato Basil Soup

Preparation Time: 30 minutes

Serves: 6

Calories: 180

Ingredients:

6 tomatoes, diced

1 onion, chopped

3 cloves garlic, minced

4 cups vegetable broth

1 cup fresh basil leaves

2 tablespoons tomato paste

1 teaspoon dried oregano

Salt and pepper

2 tablespoons olive oil

Method of Preparation:

1. In a pot, sauté onions and garlic in olive oil until translucent.
2. Add tomatoes, tomato paste, vegetable broth, oregano, salt, and pepper.

3. Simmer until tomatoes break down.
4. Blend the soup until smooth.
5. Stir in fresh basil and adjust seasoning.
6. Serve hot, garnished with additional basil if desired.

Kale and Potato Soup

Preparation Time: 35 minutes

Serves: 5

Calories: 220

Ingredients:

3 potatoes, diced

1 bunch kale, chopped

1 onion, diced

3 cloves garlic, minced

6 cups vegetable broth

1 teaspoon thyme

1 teaspoon paprika

Salt and pepper

2 tablespoons olive oil

Method of Preparation:

1. In a large pot, sauté onions and garlic in olive oil until softened.
2. Add potatoes, kale, vegetable broth, thyme, paprika, salt, and pepper. Simmer until potatoes are tender.
3. Adjust seasoning, and serve hot.

High-Protein Cabbage Soup

Preparation Time: 40 minutes

Serves: 6

Calories: 250

Ingredients:

1 small head of cabbage, shredded

1-pound lean ground turkey

1 onion, diced

3 carrots, sliced

3 celery stalks, chopped

4 cups low-sodium chicken broth

1 can (14 oz) diced tomatoes, undrained

2 cloves garlic, minced

1 teaspoon dried thyme

Salt and pepper

1 cup cooked quinoa (as a protein-rich alternative)

Method of Preparation:

1. In a large pot, brown the ground turkey over medium heat until cooked through.
2. Drain excess fat.
3. Add onions and garlic, sauté until fragrant.
4. Add carrots, celery, and cabbage.
5. Cook until vegetables are slightly softened.
6. Pour in chicken broth and add diced tomatoes with their juice. Stir in thyme, salt, and pepper.
7. Simmer for 20-25 minutes or until vegetables are tender.
8. Stir in cooked quinoa before Serves.

High-Protein Leek and Potato Soup

Preparation Time: 35 minutes

Serves: 4

Calories: 280

Ingredients:

3 leeks, sliced

4 large potatoes, peeled and diced

1 onion, chopped

2 cloves garlic, minced

4 cups vegetable broth

1 cup low-fat Greek yogurt (as a protein-rich alternative to cream)

1 teaspoon dried thyme

Salt and pepper

2 tablespoons olive oil

Chopped fresh chives for garnish

Method of Preparation:

In a large pot, heat olive oil over medium heat.

Add onions, leeks, and garlic. Sauté until softened.

1. Add potatoes, vegetable broth, and thyme.
2. Bring to a boil, then reduce heat and simmer until potatoes are tender.
3. Using an immersion blender, blend the soup until smooth.
4. Stir in Greek yogurt, salt, and pepper.
5. Simmer for an additional 5 minutes.
6. Garnish with chopped fresh chives before Serves.

Cauliflower Soup

Preparation Time: 30 minutes.

Serves: 4.

Calories: 120

Ingredients:

1 medium-sized cauliflower, chopped

1 onion, diced

2 cloves garlic, minced

4 cups vegetable broth

1 cup unsweetened almond milk

1 tablespoon olive oil

Salt and pepper

1/4 cup nutritional yeast (optional, for added flavor)

Method of Preparation:

1. In a large pot, sauté onions and garlic in olive oil until softened.
2. Add cauliflower, vegetable broth, almond milk, salt, and pepper.
3. Bring to a boil, then simmer until cauliflower is tender.
4. Use an immersion blender to puree the soup until smooth.
5. Stir in nutritional yeast if desired, and adjust seasoning to taste.
6. Serve hot, garnished with fresh herbs if desired.

Asparagus and Pea Soup

Preparation Time: 25 minutes.

Serves: 4

Calories: 150

Ingredients:

1 bunch asparagus, trimmed and chopped

1 cup frozen peas

1 onion, finely chopped

2 cloves garlic, minced

4 cups vegetable broth

1 tablespoon olive oil

1/2 cup plain Greek yogurt

Salt and pepper

Fresh lemon juice for a zesty touch

Method of Preparation:

1. In a large pot, sauté onions and garlic in olive oil until translucent.
2. Add asparagus, peas, and vegetable broth.
3. Bring to a boil, then simmer until vegetables are tender.
4. Use an immersion blender to puree the soup until creamy.
5. Stir in Greek yogurt, salt, and pepper.
6. Adjust seasoning to taste.
7. Finish with a squeeze of fresh lemon juice before Serves.

CONCLUSION

In conclusion, beyond the enticing aromas and tantalizing tastes, the significance of protein in muscle development, satiety, and overall well-being has been underscored.

This cookbook isn't just about satisfying hunger; it's about nurturing your body with the essential building blocks it craves for optimal functioning.

Whether you're an athlete aiming to enhance performance, a fitness enthusiast sculpting your physique, or an individual simply seeking sustained energy, the recipes within these pages are crafted with you in mind.

My culinary exploration has not only celebrated the rich diversity of soups but also aimed to redefine the perception of protein-centric meals.

It is evident that soup isn't just a warm, comforting dish; it's a versatile way for crafting nutrient-dense, high-protein creations that cater to various tastes and dietary needs.

Finally, I've highlighted ingredients that serve as protein powerhouses, offering you a chance to appreciate the synergy of taste and nutrition.

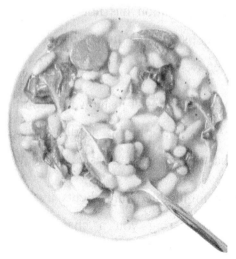

Made in the USA
Monee, IL
15 May 2025

17539529R00046